You're Special

You're Special

EXPLORING

GOD'S LOVE

FOR HIS

CHILDREN

Julia Giles

**kevin
mayhew**

First published in 2002 by
KEVIN MAYHEW LTD
Buxhall, Stowmarket, Suffolk IP14 3BW
Email: info@kevinmayhewltd.com

9 8 7 6 5 4 3 2 1 0

ISBN 1 84003 984 1
Catalogue No 1500546

Cover design by Angela Selfe
Illustrated by Sharon Kulesa
Edited and typeset by Elisabeth Bates
Printed and bound in Great Britain

Contents

About the author

Julia Giles (42) was born in Lincolnshire and has spent most of her life in and around the area. A local newspaper journalist, her life changed completely after the 'close encounters with God' which followed the births of her two children.

Nine years ago, following the birth of her second child, Julia became a Sunday School teacher and began a process of learning more of God through her own and other people's children. Many of these poems stem from her close connections with children, both her own and other people's! Many have been specifically written as a result of her own periods of emotional and mental crisis and one of their main uses prior to publication has been as encouragement for those who experience deep mental suffering. In them, as well as in herself, Julia discovered a desperate need for self-worth and identity.

She says: 'There was a turning point in my Christian life when I realised that I could accept that the promises in this book were real and were spoken to me personally. It made such a big difference to my own life to feel God thought of me as special . . . and I hope this book can contribute to helping others in the same way, whatever their age.'

Introduction: a simple path

When I began to compile this book, it was a book for children; as I went on, it became a book for children and families. Very naturally too, it was a book for Sunday Schools, for art workshops and for schools. It was only as it developed and changed that I recognised that it was a book for all ages – a book to build up confidence and self-worth, perhaps even to help us to recognise who we are. Most of all, however, this book gives people of all ages permission to be children.

We live in a world that, sadly, forces our children and ourselves into grown-upness long before we are ready for it, a world where innocence and dependence on God are out of fashion. The purpose of this book is to throw such silliness away and to get on with the serious business of coming to God as children and accepting wholeheartedly the love he offers us and the value he places upon us. We are special to him, no matter what we do or say, and there are times when we need to know that without a shadow of a doubt. When the rest of the world rejects, he never, ever does so.

Part of the problem is that we live in a world that makes God horribly, horribly complex and the path to him terribly confusing, when it really isn't that way at all. We do not understand God and cannot because, as he tells us, his ways are so very much higher than our own. But, when Jesus came to earth, he was a wonderful expression of God's enormous love and forgiveness. He pointed the way. A simple path. And it is his words that came to mind again and again as this book was put together . . .

Let the children come to me, and do not hinder them, for the kingdom of God belongs to such as these. I tell you the truth, anyone who will not receive the kingdom of God as a little child will never enter it.
(Mark 10:15)

So here's a simple book with several simple messages that I have needed and that many people need at this time. Be simple. God loves you. Listen to your children. Be a child yourself. Know that, when the world knocks you down, God builds you up. Get to know him and, in doing so, maybe you can begin to find out who you really are.

Finally, take the ideas in this book. Get creative. Don't worry about how 'professional' the final result might be. Do things as differently as you want to do them. If the pages are too small, roll out some old wallpaper and cut and stick.

In our creativity, we draw closer to the Creator. And there are no limitations for him, no walls. Many of the ideas in this book can be used for group art-work, from making treasure chests out of cardboard boxes to designing babies! Think big or think small, it doesn't matter. And remember . . . you're special. We all are!

JULIA GILES

Sketched out – with love

I have loved you with an everlasting love;
I have drawn you with loving kindness.
(Jeremiah 31:3)

That's what God himself says in his Word, the Bible, to his people. It's a message, given through God's prophet, Jeremiah, that sparks off our imagination. Imagine God with pencil in hand, drawing you. Well, it's true! You belong to him too. He created you, and naturally he has to be the best artist ever!

So draw that hand as it draws you. With all of us, there are parts God sometimes rubs out and draws afresh. Nevertheless, he loves you the way you are and he's right there with you, touching you with his colours, refining you each day, with his everlasting love!

Words to write on your heart

You're original! You're the only one of you there is. God created you and calls you by name. He knew you and the plans he had for you even before you were born. In the book of Isaiah, this is how he puts it to his people –

Fear not, for I have redeemed you. I have summoned you by name;
you are mine.
(Isaiah 43:1)

In John's Gospel, Jesus himself puts it even more clearly – *'For God so loved the world that he gave his one and only Son, that whoever believes in him should not perish but have eternal life'* (3:16). If you think about this single verse and replace 'the world' with your own name, it will give you a special knowledge of how much God really does love you!

You're special

No matter how small you may feel
in this great, aching universe –
you're special.
No matter how hard it may be
to lift your head from the pillow
and start a new day –
you're special.
And, when the world closes in,
when it seems there's no escape,
remember . . .
you're special
to the One who made you that way!

Sign your name across my heart

Draw a heart and write some special words on it. Write the word 'Jesus' – imagine he signs it there. There couldn't be a greater sign of being loved. Perhaps you could use some words from the Bible that encourage you, like the verses from John or Isaiah. Or you could simply write . . . 'I'm special' or 'God loves me'. Use your imagination. That's what it's there for!

God – with knitting needles

The thought that God knows us absolutely and completely, even down to when we sit down and stand up; every thought that passes through our minds; every word that is about to be on our tongues, could be viewed as oppressive. Unless, through the mercy and forgiveness of Jesus, we really know him fully. Then it actually becomes a consolation, a comfort, a source of wonderment that he should really take so much trouble with us! Psalm 139, written by King David, the ancestor of Jesus himself, is one of the greatest sources of this type of comfort . . . *'For you created my inmost being,'* it tells us. *'You knit me together in my mother's womb'* (verse 13).

We've seen God as artist . . . but what about God with his knitting needles? Can you imagine him – even draw him – knitting you together, before you were born? Now, there's a challenge!

Knit together and labelled with love!

God knits us together. He has a plan for us all. *'All the days ordained for me were written in your book, long before one of them came to be'* says Psalm 139 (verse 16). He has the plan. Parents don't. So, tempted as we are, as parents, to take charge of our children's lives, we should remember we can give them the best starting points with him, give them guidance too; but they have to make their own mistakes.

This poem was inspired by the thought of a newborn baby, addressing mother and father. The particular baby in question was my own – but it could just as easily be yours, whatever his/her age!

Precious gift

I am your baby,
the most precious gift ever given.
Your part in creation.
Please, take care of me.

Clothe me and feed me.
But, I beg you, give me more.
For I need to know who I am,
my place in the world.

Help me to discover the joy of life.
For a part of me is an empty page,
and it is you who will write upon it.
You are so important in beginning my story.

Whatever you write will become a part of me.
So give me the gift of innocence.
Show me the beauty of earth,
and, please, don't forget to tell me of heaven.

Teach me the value of true wisdom.
Show me how to love through your love,
and help me to know where to turn
when I am crying out for help.

I beg you, do not give me
everything my heart desires.
For there must be room for imagination.
Besides, I must learn that life is not always easy.

As my story goes on, I will become my own person.
You must allow me to take up the pen.
You must watch me make mistakes,
even though it may give you pain.

For it is not for you to judge how my tale will unfold.
It may be a romance, an adventure,
a classic studied by all those who love beauty.
But even you cannot keep some tragedy from its pages.

So many people will inhabit my world.
Some will be introduced by you.
Others I will find for myself.
I will make my own friends; but pray my enemies are few.

And there is One whose story is more important
than any you or I could ever write.
The One you must help me to discover . . .
in each page, each chapter, each line.

For he is the greatest hero our world will ever know.
The Saviour who is there to hold me, to carry me.
To bear me each day along the path
that leads to our Father's arms.

Please, please . . .
help me to find a friend in Jesus.

Jesus said, 'Let the little children come to me, and do not hinder them,
for the kingdom of God belongs to such as these.'
(Luke 18:16)

Held in a special way

We are always surrounded by God's love, but there are times when we experience a very special awareness of it, like being wrapped in a wonderful blanket, or perhaps, in modern terms, a duvet! This poem describes that feeling.

But it needs one thing! Could you imagine and design on the following page the pattern on God's duvet? What colours would it be? What would it show to us? Is it possible to show the loveliness of being held in God's love in that design? Would it show his everlasting arms, as described in the book of Deuteronomy, or perhaps resting in the shadow of his wings, as David speaks of it in Psalm 91? Or would you just show the wonder of his creation in some form or other?

God's duvet

Wrapped in your love.
Wrapped safe and secure.
O Lord,
could I ever want more?
Safe in the softness of your caring.
Safe and loved – reborn in the sharing
of care upon care,
of hurt and of pain.
And, in the hurt,
to feel your love again and again!

And I am for ever
wrapped in your love,
enraptured in love.
Covered, safe, secure.
Could I ever . . .
could I ever want more?

A new creation – God's duvet!

My design . . .

These verses may give some inspiration . . .

He will cover you with his feathers and under his wings you will find refuge.
(Psalm 91:4)

The eternal God is your refuge, and underneath are the everlasting arms.
(Deuteronomy 33:27)

Little treasures

If we have periods of our lives when we feel a little on the low side, or as if the world is very much against us, it is essential to recognise our true value. Here are a few little nuggets to help us to realise that we really are precious, beautiful and lots of other things too. Little treasures, in fact. Really!

Precious to me

God told me, 'You're a jewel,'
but why should I believe?
After all, I'm only me . . .
No, I couldn't quite believe.

God told me, 'You're a treasure!'
'Oh, come on, God,' I said.
He says the strangest things.
I hear them in my head.

'You were made to shine,' God said.
But why should I believe?
After all, I'm only me.
No, I couldn't quite believe.

A funny thing God did to me.
He showed me it was true.
Yes, I sparkled. Yes, I shone –
and so did others too.

So God said, 'You are my jewel.'
And, yes, I do believe.
It's when I look at others,
I can't help but believe!

Imagine . . . a treasure chest! Not some strange, modern plastic version but the kind of beautifully made treasure chest with brass hinges that you would see in tales of pirates; the kind of chest that in reality belonged to princes or kings of mighty empires.

In that way, maybe we can imagine God's treasure chest. Only, on this particular chest – because it is the treasure chest of the King of kings and it contains his children – is a label and this label, tied firmly to the chest, says simply . . . LOVED. Draw this label tied to the chest below.

Now draw 'jewels' in the treasure chest. Yourself, of course. But not just yourself. Try putting your brothers and sisters in there; your parents and grandparents. Then . . . the biggest challenge of all: put someone in there that you really struggle to get along with. Make a point of whispering a prayer for them. Yes, believe it or not, God loves *them*.

Come as a child . . .
and keep the child inside!

Well, I said at the beginning this wasn't just a children's book. Here's a selection for older 'kids', bearing in mind that Jesus tells us specifically to come to God as children. What does that mean to us? Being fun-loving, being open, enthusiastic . . . perhaps even a little vulnerable. I suppose it also means being pretty awkward and nasty at times, letting things show, being honest. These poems are very personal to me. But that doesn't mean that they can't strike chords in others.

Why me?

God, you're a mighty Creator,
the best there could ever be.
But daily, Lord, I'm astounded.
Oh, why did you create me?

Words that flow,
thoughts that explode,
swamped in your Living Water.
Praying, loving,
laughing, crying.
Glad always that I am your daughter!

And, Lord, the colours shine on your brush.
The notes, they flow from your hands.
You're potter, artist, craftsman.
Oh, how can I understand?

And your thoughts are so very much higher than mine,
the highest there could ever be.
So, Lord, tell me, 'cause I am astounded.
Oh, why did **you** *create* **me***?*

'For my thoughts are not your thoughts, neither are your ways my ways,' declares the Lord.
'As the heavens are higher than the earth, so are my ways higher than your ways
and my thoughts than your thoughts.' (Isaiah 55:8-9)

God's smile

How can we see God's smile
when we cannot see his face?
And how do you explain to someone
that you can feel God as he smiles on you,
as he smiles in a heart and lights up a life?

And God smiles on me today.
He wraps me in his love
and he whispers in ear and in heart.

Smile on me, Lord.
Smile on me today,
for another day I may disappoint.
But I will always find forgiveness at your feet.
And I know . . .
the smile will be renewed.

God's smile! It must be rather too big for this page to contain. But we can still draw it. Go on . . . and smile with him!

To Doris

(A message for a friend on her eightieth birthday.)

No matter how old you may be,
you are still a child to me.
No matter how many years.
No matter how many tears.
And how many fears have you faced?
You are still a child to me.

And you are so loved by me.
So cherished, so cared-for, so free . . .

So free to grow in my love.
And how you have grown, my child.
Never alone, my child.
Always, always with me.

And no matter where you may be,
you are young at heart in me.
You are . . .
another captive set free.
And you are still a child to me!

I tell you the truth, anyone who will not receive the kingdom of God like a
little child will never enter it.
(The words of Jesus, Luke 18:17)

23

Special . . . but there's room for improvement

Yes, you're special, but it's important to remember that so is everyone else. Yes, everyone, even the people who are the most irritating to you! . . . We are all made by God in his image, and we are all part of his creation. He accepts us as we are; he loves us, yes, but that doesn't mean there isn't room for improvement. So let's not get too self-important. We need to see we are just a small, if miraculous part, of his wonderful and miraculous creation! And to remember he is at the heart of all things!

Humble, yet special

You are . . .
The beauty of the skies.
The vastness of the ocean.
The love born within the heart of a newborn baby.
And I?
I am but a tiny pinprick in your world.

You are . . .
The softness of a kitten's fur.
The smile on the face of a friend.
You are the hunger pangs of the starving child.
The pain of the one who has lost their home
as the bombs begin to fall.
You are . . .
The wind, the flame, the living water.

And I?
I am but a tiny pinprick in your world.

So tiny . . . so insignificant?
No . . . so special.
Created by the One who made the stars of the night.
The beauty of the moon.
The heat of the sun.
Created, moulded,
and made, like them,
to shine!

Made to shine

Am I really made to shine? Of course. If you don't believe it, listen to the words of Jesus and then draw yourself again. You remember that first picture? There you are drawn by God himself. Here, draw yourself as he sees you through Christ . . . with his light shining through.

After all, this is what Jesus says in the Gospel of Matthew . . .

You are the light of the world. A city on a hill cannot be hidden. Neither do people light a lamp and put it under a bowl. Instead they put it on its stand and it gives light to everyone in the house. In the same way, let your light shine before men that they may see your good deeds and praise your Father in heaven. (Matthew 5:14-16)

A hundred kisses a day!

If God loves us, how does he show it? Many people are very negative about God and blame him for the troubles of the world, most of which we are responsible for ourselves. I am quite the opposite; I always find myself over-whelmed by his goodness, mercy and patience. Walking with God means his blessings come to us – sometimes we have to be very 'pure in heart', as Jesus tells us, to see that and to see him. Here's a poem written by my daughter, aged 5, which seems to sum it up.

God gives us a hundred kisses a day.
I can feel him kiss me as I pray.
God kisses the earth and sky.
He kisses me low and high.

God kisses the flowers and trees.
He hugs the insects and the bees.
He loves all the people in the world.
Every boy and every girl.

God loves us so much that he gave us his Son.
He died for us; that is what he has done.
And I kiss God and God kisses me.
I love him so much for setting me free.

Blessed are the pure in heart,
for they shall see God.
(The words of Jesus, Matthew 5:8)

Going our own way

This isn't just a children's book and, even if it was, there has to be honesty. The honest thing is, we are not always well-behaved all the time. That's impossible, unless we live in total isolation – and even then it's almost impossible! There's always a battle that goes on inside. We want to go our own way and God wants us to go his. That's why he sent Jesus to us – to show us the way. To cross the great divide that separates us!

So, we wander away, like silly children, which is what we are at times, or like lost sheep. And here's a story to tell our children and a story that we might just recognise as being us. Sometimes it can be us for a long time and sometimes just for a little while, but there are very few of us who can honestly say it's never, ever been us!

Jesus said: 'There was once a man who had two sons. The younger one said to him, "Father, give me my share of the property now." So the man divided his property between his two sons.

'After a few days, the younger son sold his part of the property and left home with the money. He went to a country far away where he wasted his money in reckless living. He spent everything he had. Then, a severe famine spread over that country and he was left without a thing. So he went to work for one of the citizens of that country, who sent him out to his farm to take care of the pigs. He wished he could fill himself with the bean pods the pigs ate, but no one gave him anything to eat. At last, he came to his senses and said: "All my father's hired workers have more than they can eat, and here I am about to starve! I will give up and go to my father and say, 'Father, I have sinned against God and against you. I am no longer fit to be called your son; treat me as one of your hired workers.'" So he got up and started back to his father.

'He was still a long way from home when his father saw him; his heart was filled with pity, and he ran, threw his arms around his son, and kissed him.

'"Father," the son said. "I have sinned against God and against you. I am no longer fit to be called your son." But the father called his servants. "Hurry!" he said. "Bring the best robe and put it on him. Put a ring on his finger and shoes on his feet. Then, go and get the prize calf and kill it, and let us celebrate with a feast. For this son of mine was dead, but now he is alive; he was lost but now he has been found." And so the feasting began.'
(Luke 15:11-24)

Many of us feel guilty about not doing the things we should or having done the things we shouldn't without even realising it. That's why we need to know stories like this one, from Jesus, and to understand that all we have to do is go back, turn around, say sorry and we can start again. Jesus points the way for us all in this story . . . straight towards the arms of the Father. And see how that father runs towards his son as he returns home; how he throws his arms around him and kisses him, 'his heart filled with pity'. Can we see that as a picture of God himself and his love for us all?

The prodigal daughter

We're not perfect. None of us gets it totally right all the time. For those who feel they ought to, perhaps this poem – a personal view of a 'prodigal' (me) – might help a little.

And Father, you stood waiting this morning.
Open arms.
Ready to run towards me.
Garment of praise in hand.
I, weary and shop-soiled,
filthy garment,
well, I had been in the pig-sty . . .
again,
wandered off the road once more.

I stood . . .
too dirty for your majestic courts.
Too hurt, too damaged
to climb red-carpeted stairs to your door.
Weak knees weaker than ever.
Spent . . .
again!

'I'm so sorry, Lord!' I cry.
Again.
You must be sick of hearing it by now.
Surprised you don't just stuff divine cotton-wool in your ears.
Put away that red carpet
for good.

How can you look on me,
stained as I am?
How can I dirty that carpet with filthy feet
muddy from the mire?

No, he has to carry me again, doesn't he?
As always.
Bearer of sin, bearer of pain.
I certainly don't know how he can bear me!!

Thank you, Father.
Thank you that you gave us your Son.
Light in the darkness.
Purity in unloveliness.
Kissing a guilty world, a guilty people
with your perfect love.

Thank you for running to meet me
as I finally climb the stairs.
I understand why the carpet is so red now.
Must be the blood he washes me in.

Thank you, Lord.
Thank you that I stand again in your presence,
unworthy as I am.

It's so light here! I had almost forgotten.
. . . can we have another celebration?

Jesus said: 'I am the way, the truth, and the life.
No one comes to the Father except through me.' (John 14:6)

He really delights in me?

Prodigal? Wandering? Sometimes just feeling down. Sometimes exhausted from doing too much or simply doing the wrong things. As someone who tends to do too much too quickly, I sometimes find that somehow I have managed to abandon the housework, husband, children and the cat in the process! At such times, the guilt sets in. I have to readjust my sights and remember that God not only loves me, he actually *delights* in me!

And, of course, the same applies to us all. I won't bother to outline my own shortcomings as wife and mother in prose. This poem says it all . . . and perhaps a little for others too. It is one of a number based on David's psalms, and its roots are Psalm 18:19. *'He brought me out into a spacious place; he rescued me because he delighted in me!'* It really is an awesome thought!

You delight in **me**?
Well, that's rather a large thought to take on board!
I shall consider it today.
That you, my God, delights in **me**!

I shall consider it and let you know later
if I think you ought to . . .

I mean . . . **me**?
Housework incomplete.
Life-plan in disarray.
Too many bills to pay.
Shouting at the kids,
though not as much as I used to
without you.

Poetry piled up in tray.
Filing system in disarray.
Have to sort it out again . . .
but not today.
Please, not today.

Ironing still left from Sunday.
Hoovering to do from Monday.
Cat still to be fed.
And look at the state of those beds!
Not to mention my head.

You delight in **me?**
Let me think about it carefully . . .

Washing still on the line
from three days ago.
Rained on again!

And how long is it
since I had a bath?
Oh, and when did I last eat
a vegetable?
Come to think of it,
what is a vegetable?
Atrocious example for the kids.

Right, think positive!
Today I have read your words,
though probably not enough.
We have shared various conversations,
though I have to confess,
like this one, they're a little one-sided!

Naturally,
I have written more poetry
to go in the writing-up tray!
And . . . I have tried to let the light of you
shine through.
So maybe,
just maybe,
I have done a little.

Anyway,
thanks for the spacious place.
It just looks a bit of a mess at the moment!

What?
You **really** delight in **me!!?**

Celebrate our differences!

We all go through silly phases in our lives that we can either look back on and upset ourselves about or treat with humour. I went through a phase where the world knocked me down and God told me I was special. Great! The trouble was, I then began to think everyone else should be like me. Whoops! It's a big problem in the world today – conventional people annoy the unconventional; serious people are annoyed by the light-hearted; noisy people are a pain to the quiet ones . . . and *vice-versa*.

But God made us all differently and he wants us to make the best of our talents and what we are. He wants us to recognise that he delights in us and in others too. He loves our differences. So how about seeing that in terms of a garden? God is, after all, a wonderful gardener . . . and we see that most of all when Jesus speaks of him in the Gospel of John, Chapter 15: *'I am the true vine and my Father is the gardener.'* Jesus goes on to describe how God refines us to bring us into full bloom and how we need to stay firmly attached to 'the vine'. It's a beautiful passage, and it can be a beautiful garden. Perhaps a rainbow garden!

The rainbow garden

If I were a flower, what would I be?
Oh, I'd be a daffodil, wild and free.
Shouting out sunshine, blaring out the Good News.
Yes, a daffodil's the flower that I would choose.

If you were a flower, what would you be
if God gave you a place in his flower bed?
The delicate violet seeking the sun?
The daisy just raising its sunshine head?

Would you be a carnation? Would you be a rose?
Sweet-scented or just getting up someone's nose?
Perhaps you'd be the butter in a buttercup
or the purest white of the tiny snowdrop.

Oh, there are so very many to choose.
Strident or quiet, tiny or tall.
Reds, purples and greens, yellows and blues,
blowing their trumpets or acting quite small.

You see, God is the gardener and he loves each one.
Bathes all of his flowers in the warmth of his sun.
Waters and nurtures his plants from above.
Brings them into blossom through the power of his love.

So hold out your hand and he'll open the gate.
He'll show you the wonders of what you can be.
No reason to pause; no need to be late.
Walk into the rainbow; walk in and run free!

Get the idea? You're a flower. OK, it might be difficult to imagine or it might not. But, if you *are* a flower, then what sort are you? There's space here to think, or even to draw.

God loves the unconventional too

At times, I meet some very unconventional people who always lead me to the conclusion that they are much loved by God (along with the conventional ones of course!). The unconventional are sometimes the most imaginative – they are the ones who might feel God's flower bed doesn't include them because, as a flower, they haven't been invented yet.

There seems little room for imagination today. We live in a world that deals so much in knowledge and facts, rather than the things we cannot see or classify. The world likes to label both people and emotions. But, like love, thankfully, we cannot classify imagination; it is miraculous! So this poem celebrates the imagination of the Master Artist, God, and the imagination that is within us all to different degrees.

The rainbow flower

So God decided on a brand-new plan.
Sitting, rainbow-pen in hand,
it took him a while – at least an hour –
to design his very own rainbow flower.

Sparkling and dancing, the flower of your dreams.
So bright, so amazing, yellows and greens.
Purples and reds, pinks and blues.
So many shadings, so many hues.

Petals so soft, leaves blown in the wind.
A flower you'd always choose as a friend.
One minute a sparkle, one minute one colour.
Then, turning and blowing – look, there's another!

A rainbow flower! My word, how amazing!
Enough to set the heart of each child ablazing.
And God smiles on the beauty of the rainbow flower.
What beauty! What promise! The dazzle! The power!

Such a wonder of wonders is God's creation!
And the greatest of wonders . . . IMAGINATION!

A rainbow flower - amazing thought?

What do you think the amazing rainbow flower looks like? Could it be you? Use that imagination and just draw it! God doesn't expect us all to be master artists, but we can all use our imaginations.

I like the colour 'you'

Yes, we are all creative but, of course, some of us are especially gifted. I was helping a teacher in an art lesson, using poetry as inspiration for the creative talents of some 6-year-olds. Having completed Vincent Van Gogh's 'Starry Night' masterpiece in multi-coloured pieces of wool, I felt we had really done something original!

Left with a little time on our hands, we looked at the vivid colours in the original picture and, playing for time, I asked the youngsters about their favourite colours. They gave a multitude of answers, but it was one particularly small boy who had been reciting short verses of his own original poetry all afternoon who gave me a wonderful memory and a wonderful slice of inspiration. Coming over to me and fingering my pastel pink and lilac dress, he looked up at me and said in unforgettable tones, 'I like the colour "you".'

Arriving home, I was inspired to write the following, which we used in a subsequent art session.

I like the colour blue

I like the colour blue
and I like the colour 'you'.
and whatever colour you might be,
I like the colours that I see.
Yes, whatever you may be today,
I'd simply like to say . . .
that I like the colour 'you'.

And I like the colour 'you',
whether orange, pink or blue.
'Cause I think you are a star –
that must be what you are.
The gold shining in the blue . . .
yes, I like the colour 'you'.

Do you like the colour 'me'?
'Cause I think that I can be
a starry night or sunflower,
a rainbow after shower.
Green, orange, yellow, blue . . .
lovely colours, just like you!

What colour are you today?

Some people might say abstract art – just splashing colours on a page – doesn't look like anything. But what it can do is simply reflect who we are and what we feel. As someone who just cannot draw, I find that I can show things in this way. So what colour are you? You could be anything from joyful yellow, to passionate red or calm blue.

Use this space to scribble, to think and then perhaps it could be time for a big brush and a large piece of paper. Enjoy it. You might be surprised at the result and the feeling of freedom it gives.

Held and moulded by a loving God

This book was written to encourage people. First, to encourage them that they are special, then to encourage them that they can come to God quite simply as children in need of love and forgiveness, and find exactly that. What is encouraging too is to know that we are held in his hands. That, despite the way things might look, he has plans for us. From cradle to grave. The image of God's hand is overwhelming in this collection. We can see God in so many, many ways, always using his hands to hold us, shape us, build us up and form us. As Master Artist, as gardener, builder, architect, the conductor of an orchestra, a musician stroking the strings. We can see him, along with the Prophet Isaiah and others, as the potter with the clay in his hands.

Who was it who said, 'God loves us the way we are but he loves us far too much to leave us that way'? This poem reminds me of that statement. God cares for us so much that he wants the best for us – therefore, he changes us in many, many ways. Sometimes it's delightful, sometimes painful but it's all part of his plan for our lives.

'The potter and the clay' was written in what seems another lifetime to me. Sometimes, the first poetry is very simple. Then we think it is too simple and it is tempting to discard it. It's a mistake. It is so very important, because it is fresh and easily understandable, and it is important not to become too complex. The world suffers at times in its over-complexity.

The potter and the clay

Lord, you are the potter.
You stand here at the wheel.
And, Lord, I ask, please mould me
in everything I feel.

Lord, you are the potter.
Here I stand, the clay.
And, Lord I ask, please mould me,
change me with each new day.

Take my heart and give it wings.
My soul, prepare for flight.
A heart that's so in love with you.
Keep heaven in my sight.

Not a heaven above me.
Not a heaven of rest.
Just the heaven in my heart.
A love for the oppressed.

Lord, you are the potter.
I know I'm in your hands.
My God, my Saviour, dearest friend.
The One who understands.

Always guided by you.
Resting, safe, secure.
Caressed and moulded by your hand.
Loved for evermore.

Yet, O Lord, you are our Father. We are the clay, you are the potter; we are all the work of your hand. (Isaiah 64:8)

We are very fortunate if we have access to a potter's wheel to work on. If you do, why not consider this aspect of God as you work with your own handful of clay?

For others, a lump of plasticine or something similar is brilliant. Why not mould a model of yourself, and think of the loving care with which God does the same thing!

Is there any other way?

So . . . we come to God, through his Son, not as silly grown-ups who are always asking pointless questions and finding rather pointless answers. We come not as people of logic who are only prepared to see what is in front of them. Nor do we come as people who think it is staggeringly mature to probe things in depth and find alternative answers . . . and confuse ourselves and others in the process. We come as children and coming as children is a very joyful thing to do!

If we doubt, we question. We seek more information. From others perhaps. But, best of all from the One who really knows it all. We see beyond the logical . . . and that's when we see miracles! Because God isn't logical in the slightest. Otherwise, why would he have so much patience with us?

I find many people who want to be in charge of their own lives and certainly don't want God to plan them or Jesus to be in the driving seat. Personally, as I am hopeless at being in charge of mine and have no sense of direction, I can't think of anything better! It's a great relief for me to know that of course I can make my own decisions; of course I can be me and be much-loved just as I am but, ultimately, the One who really knows what he's doing is in charge, leading the way.

Some time ago, I watched an episode of the much-loved British television comedy series, *Last of the Summer Wine*. For many years, three aged but playful companions had become a part of family life with their wanderings and their fun and games in the Yorkshire Dales. Sadly, this was the episode in which the lovable, irresponsible and fun-loving Compo walked the hills in his wellies for the last time. Months previously I had not shed a tear on hearing the news of actor Bill Owen's death. He was not a part of my life. The character he played was; Compo was dead, and I cried for hours.

What stuck in my mind most of all was a comment made by Compo's companion, Cleggy . . . along the lines of . . . *'Well, he says "Come as a child", and he always did.'* He was, of course, referring to those core words of advice from Jesus to his disciples. In an effort to protect their tired Saviour, they try to turn away those who bring their babies and young children to him, but he rebukes them with these memorable words: *'Let the little children come to me and do not hinder them, for the kingdom of God belongs to such as these. I tell you the truth, anyone who will not receive the kingdom of God like a little child will never enter it . . .'*

Struck afresh by the importance of these words and the death of a character who epitomised 'the child in the man', I wrote the following:

Come as a child / Elegy to Compo

'Come as a child,' he says,
and as a child, I come.
I hear the voice of the One
who heals the blind, the deaf, the dumb.
'Come as a child,' he says.
And as a child, I come.

'Come as a child who longs to run.
Come as the child you are to me.
Come as the child who sits at my feet.
Come as a child,' he says.
And as a child I come.

'Come as a child and be free.
Come as a child to me.
Come as a child to laugh and play.
Come as a child today.'

There is always room, always time.
For a child is never turned away.
'Come as a child,' I hear him say.
And as a child I come . . .

Is there any other way?

41

Appendix

The little children and Jesus
Mark 10:13-16

People were bringing little children to Jesus to have him touch them, but the disciples rebuked them. When Jesus saw this, he was indignant. He said to them, 'Let the little children come to me, and do not hinder them, for the kingdom of God belongs to such as these. I tell you the truth, anyone who will not receive the kingdom of God like a little child will never enter it.' And he took the children in his arms, put his hands on them and blessed them.

The Words of Jesus: God the gardener
John 15:1-18

I am the real vine and my Father is the gardener. He breaks off every branch in me that does not bear fruit, and he prunes every branch that does bear fruit, so that it will be clean and bear more fruit. You have been made clean already by the teaching I have given you. Remain united to me and I will remain united to you. A branch cannot bear fruit by itself; it can do so only if it remains in the vine. In the same way, you cannot bear fruit unless you remain in me.

I am the vine and you are the branches. Whoever remains in me and I in him will bear much fruit; for you can do nothing without me. Whoever does not remain in me is thrown out like a branch and dries up; such branches are gathered up and thrown into the fire where they are burnt. If you remain in me and my words remain in you, then you will ask for anything you wish and you shall have it. My Father's glory is shown by your bearing much fruit; and in this way you become my disciples. I love you, just as the Father loves me; remain in my love. If you obey my commands, you will remain in my love, just as I have obeyed my Father's commands and remain in his love.

I have told you this so that my joy may be in you and that your joy may be complete. My commandment is this: love one another, just as I love you. The greatest love a person can have for his friends is to give his life for them. And you are my friends if you do what I command you. I do not call you servants any longer, because servants do not know what their master is doing. Instead, I call you friends, because I have told you everything I have heard from my

Father. You did not choose me; I chose you and appointed you to go and bear much fruit, the kind of fruit that endures. And so the Father will give you whatever you ask of him in my name. This then is what I command you: love one another.

The Beatitudes
Matthew 5:1–12

Now when Jesus saw the crowds, he went up on a mountainside and sat down. His disciples came to him and he began to teach them, saying:

'Blessed are the poor in spirit, for theirs is the kingdom of heaven.
Blessed are those who mourn, for they will be comforted.
Blessed are the meek, for they will inherit the earth.
Blessed are those who hunger and thirst for righteousness, for they will be filled.
Blessed are the merciful, for they will be shown mercy.
Blessed are the pure in heart, for they will see God.
Blessed are the peacemakers, for they will be called sons of God.
Blessed are those who are persecuted because of righteousness, for theirs is the kingdom of heaven.

Blessed are you when people insult you, persecute you and falsely say all kinds of evil against you because of me. Rejoice and be glad, because great is your reward in heaven, for in the same way they persecuted the prophets who were before you.'

Psalm 139:1-18
(Written by King David)

O Lord, you have searched me and you know me.
You know when I sit and when I rise;
* you perceive my thoughts from afar.*
You discern my going out and my lying down;
* you are familiar with all my ways.*
Before a word is on my tongue,
* you know it completely, O Lord.*

You hem me in – behind and before.
You have laid your hand upon me.
Such knowledge is too wonderful for me, too lofty to attain.

Where can I go from your Spirit?
Where can I flee from your presence?
If I go up to the heavens, you are there.
If I make my bed in the depths, you are there.
If I rise on the wings of the dawn,
* if I settle on the far side of the sea,*
* even there your hand will guide me,*
* your right hand will hold me fast.*

If I say, 'Surely the darkness will hide me
* and the light become night around me,'*
* even the darkness will not be dark to you;*
* the night will shine like the day, for darkness is as light to you.*

For you created my inmost being;
* you knit me together in my mother's womb.*
I praise you because I am fearfully and wonderfully made;
* your works are wonderful. I know that full well.*
My frame was not hidden from you
* when I was made in the secret place.*
When I was woven together in the depths of the earth,
* your eyes saw my unformed body.*
All the days ordained for me were written in your book
* before one of them came to be.*

How precious to me are your thoughts, O God!
How vast is the sum of them!
Were I to count them,
* they would outnumber the grains of sand.*
When I awake, I am still with you.

Prayer

Lord,
I don't know what today holds,
but I know it holds you.
I don't know what tomorrow holds,
but I know it holds you.
I don't know the future, Lord.
But I know it is held in loving hands.
Your hands.
Amen.

Jeremiah 29:11

'For I know the plans I have for you,' declares the Lord, 'plans to prosper
you and not to harm you, plans to give you hope and a future.'

A final thought

Just think about that final prayer on page 45. Speak it aloud if you want to.

There is space below to draw around your hand. Draw around it slowly and quietly, imagining it is the hand of God himself. Then place yourself at the centre, knowing that is where you are. Alongside yourself you can place the others that you love – your family perhaps or your friends . . .

It's a good place to be and a good picture to keep in mind, always – whatever the future holds!